A BDSM Primer

What You Need To Know Before You Start To Play

Keeping it safe and Sexy

By Samantha Pall

Table of content

Introduction

If you're reading this guide, then you quite probably already have at least some idea of what BDSM is all about. That said, few people know exactly what the acronym means, or just how widely it can be applied. For that reason, before we delve into the ins, outs, hows, whats and whys of BDSM play, we're first going to take a moment to understand *exactly* what it means.

BDSM is, in fact, a compound acronym. It stands for:

- Bondage

- Discipline AND Domination

- Sadism AND Submission

- Masochism

In short, it revolves around relationships in which one person has control over the other (or where both partners take turns to be in control) and may involve the use of bondage, pain, humiliation and exotic sexual activities to make sex more exciting. For most people, this means experimenting with bondage, pain, power play and other activities in the bedroom... and perhaps even venturing to a BDSM club or play party if they feel brave enough.

Of course, the actual meaning of BDSM is different for different people. Some couples are into heavy, protocol-based play, which they enact even outside of the bedroom. Some couples just like to enjoy a little light spanking and some fun with rope. Some couples like to play in public at dungeons and play parties, while some prefer to keep it a private affair. Some people like to have more than one partner, while others choose to remain monogamous.

Although BDSM in its strictest sense is mainly about control, dominance, submission and pain, you'll probably find that as you explore you'll come across a huge range of different sexualities, preferences and types of relationship. It's up to you, in the end, to decide what BDSM means for you.

Think of this guide as a starting point for your exploration of this exciting and vibrant world. In the coming pages we'll take a look at some important safety tips which will allow you to play safely and sensibly. We'll show you how you can get your hands on some useful BDSM equipment to experiment with without breaking the bank, as well as what to do once you're ready to take the plunge and acquire some serious kit. We'll also look over some tips on bondage and roleplay to get you started.

This guide can be applied to a range of relationships... so if you think you might be interested in something a little different from a standard dominant / submissive situation, do please read on. You'll still find the tips here useful and relevant.

Done right, BDSM and kink can be life-enhancing, pleasurable and mind-expanding activities. If you're curious... if you want to explore... if you're ready to take your relationship to another level... or if you've always had a secret yearning that you've never quite fully realized... read on. This guide is for you.

Safety Tips

In this section we'll cover a number of basic safety tips that should be applicable no matter what kind of play you're interested in. Of course, it's important that you don't let safety stop here. Whenever you try a new form of play or activity, it's crucial that you take a moment to think about how you can make it safe, and what you'll do if it goes wrong. The tips here don't cover everything, but they're a good place to start.

Have A Safeword

The concept of a safeword is probably one that you've already encountered in some form or another. It's a word, agreed on before play, which – when spoken – means that the scene is over. Either partner can use a safeword to stop play whenever they feel it might be necessary: perhaps things are too intense, or perhaps they just need to make some small change before carrying on. Either way, having a safeword means that you can quickly and safely stop a scene when you need to.

The defaults safeword is "Red". You can use this, or come up with one of your own – just make sure that everyone involved in the scene knows how to stop it if necessary. That said, don't fully rely on the safeword as your only means of stopping a scene. Sometimes, in the intensity of the moment, your partner might find it difficult to speak even that simple word – so don't forget to check in regularly and make sure that they're okay.

Plan What To Do If It Goes Wrong

It's not necessary to take a full first aid course, or have a complete emergency kit in your bedroom. However, knowing what to do if something goes wrong in the course of a given activity is a must.

If you're playing with rope, plan how you're going to get in undone in an emergency. If you're playing with sharp objects, learn how to stop the bleeding from an accidental cut. Accidents WILL happen, but with a little preparation you can really mitigate the damage.

Read Around The Subject

There are many dangers involved in BDSM play, and several of them are of a nature that most people simply wouldn't expect.

If you're attempting something new, make sure to do some background reading. FetLife.com is an excellent place to get in touch with other kinksters and find out what can go wrong with any given activity.

The dangers associated with rope play are a classic example of this. Most people might think that tying someone up is a relatively safe activity... but do a little research and you'll discover that there are a multitude of dangers to take account of: nerve damage, fainting, harness hang syndrome, and so on. Only by doing some thorough background reading can you ensure that you're aware of these dangers, and take steps to mitigate them.

Don't assume that anything is safe – take the time, and do the reading... then relax and enjoy your safe and informed play.

Improvising Toys

One of the main barriers many couples encounter when it comes to exploring their kinky sides is a lack of the right equipment. Restraints, insertables and other toys can be dizzyingly expensive, and for the uninitiated it can be difficult to know what to opt for, or whether or not you enjoy a particular type of play enough to splash out on an expensive toy for it.

Don't despair, however. It's quite possible to experiment with BDSM without spending a lot of cash. And by playing with improvised equipment, you can ensure that – when you do come to purchase some toys – you'll know exactly what you want, and exactly how you plan to use it.

When it comes to improvisation, the only limits are you imagination... and safety, of course. Some of the simplest items are often the most versatile.

A belt

You can simply try a belt to use in your play to. A belt can be used for bondage, but is a great spanking tool to. A belt is not just for the hardcore BDSM. It can be used to spice things up for beginners to. Restrain you partner with the belt, then you are free to tease you partner. When you use it as a spanking tool, start slow to see how your partner reacts, you can build up the intensiveness as your partner is getting used to the feeling.

Scarves

Try introducing some scarves to the bedroom. These can be used for bondage, as well as blindfolding and a host of other activities.

Cling film

Even fairly innocuous items can be perverted. Cling film makes for an excellent bondage material

Dog collor/ lease

A dog collar and leash can help a submissive playing experience. It is also used as a indication that the person waring it is a submissive or slave in the relationship or play

Collars may used in games involving humiliation because of the connection of and pet-like status, especially when worn with the lease.

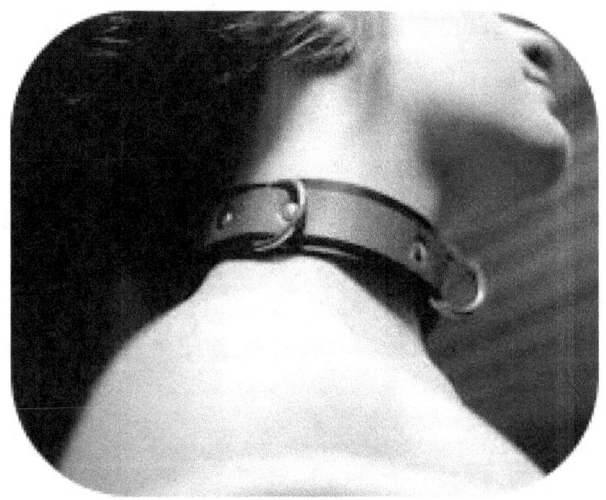

Blindfolds

A suit tie or a scarf makes a perfect blindfold. Wearing the blindfold takes out the sense of sight witch heightens the other senses. This will make every though more titillating.

Next to heightening the senses, blindfolds reduce performance pressure and inhibitions. If your partner has a blindfold one, you will feel more free to cut loose.

Candles

Candle play is a form of temperature play. It introduces a slight burning sensation to the skin.

Start with one or 2 drup first, the farther away, or higher you pour form, the cooler the wax is when it hits the body

Beware of candles too – only certain types are safe to use for wax play, while others will melt at a dangerously high temperature.

Ice cubes

Just like the candles, is ice also part of the temperature play. Using hot and cold will stimulate the neuroreceptors under your skin.

Just use ice cubes out of the freezer. You can slowly draw one along you partners body. This is especially pleasurable when your partner is in bondage or/and blindfolded.

I you really want to build up the tension, avoid the erogenous zones until the last minute.

Play with the temperature. This way you build and release loads of sexual tension.

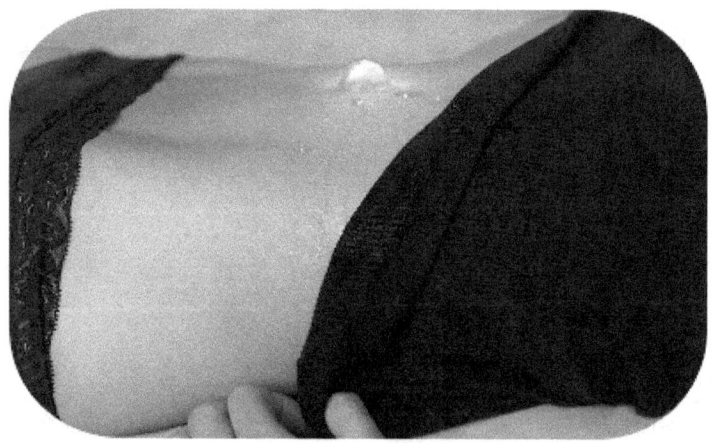

Feather duster

Use a feather duster fore tickling. You can start of the lay with a light teasing. Works well with restraints and a blindfold.

Clothespins

Get some clothespins from the laundry room, this are great to use as nipple clamps, or on other parts of the body...

Spanking tools

Wooden ruler

A tool that you can find in almost every desk. The (wooden) ruler. The ruler is perfect for some spanking punishment. Of course great to apply in kinky role-playing. A teacher disciplining a naughty student can be played perfectly with help of the ruler.

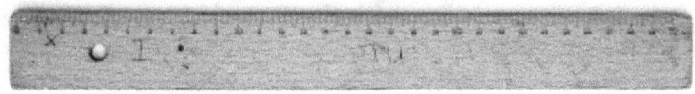

Hairbrush

The flat side of a hairbrush is a popular spanking tool in BDSM play. Hairbrush spanking was already being used in medieval times. Husbands spanked there wives with a hairbrush in a erotic and non-erotic way. Nowadays the sex thousand really matter anymore.

Submissives can take various positions to receive the speaking. A popular position is where the sub is front down across the Dom's lap.

Spatula

A spatula from the kitchen can come and in a variety of sizes and materials. These are great to use for spanking. Adjust the spatula for different pain preferences .

The hardware store

With a little imagination, a trip to the hardware store can provide you with a bounty of cheap toys.

Although the rope available at most home and garden stores is too coarse for intimate bondage, it will suffice just for testing the waters.

You can also pick up all manner of interesting rubber toys, collars, leashes and so on for anyone into pet play. Have a browse for items with an interesting texture to them – these can be used in sensation play – and keep an open mind to the possible uses of items such as duct tape, zip ties and clothes pegs.

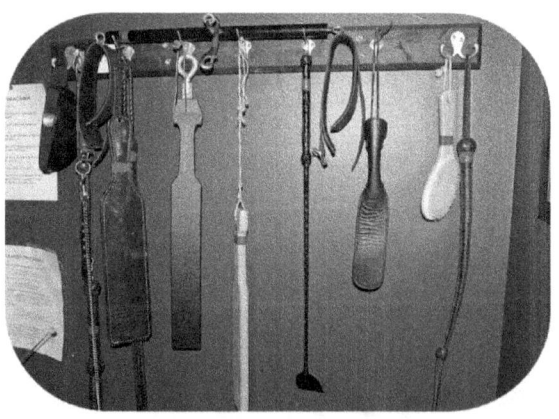

Even the fixtures and fittings of your house can be extremely useful. Take a look at your furniture, and see if you can identify any items that are the perfect height, width or depth for bondage or other play.

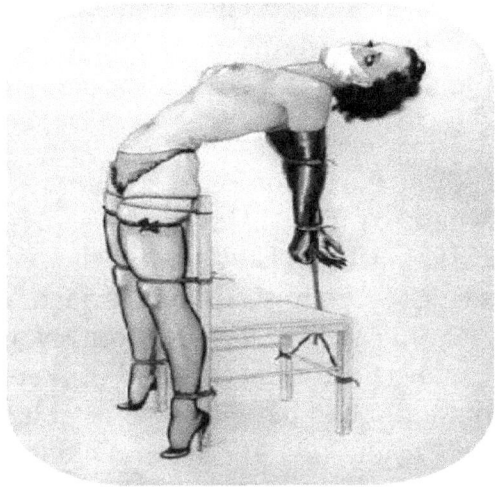

Of course, it goes without saying that when playing with improvised toys you'll be using items for something that is quite far removed from their intended purpose.

For this reason it's prudent to be extremely careful, and pace yourself when you play. Duct tape, for example, is excellent for bondage – but is far stickier than specially-manufactured bondage tape, so be careful when removing it. And be extremely wary about anything you plan to insert into your or your partner's body – only use insertables that have been especially designed for the purpose.

Other BDSM Toys

After a certain point, you will most likely find yourself wanting to purchase some toys instead of just improvising them. If you've played and experimented, you will by this stage have some idea of the kind of toy that you're after. But what's next? Where can you get your equipment from, and how can you be sure that it's of good quality.

The first of these questions is the simplest to answer. It's usually best to buy your toys in person, from a sex shop or BDSM market. Take a look at the event listings on Fetlife.com to see if there's a market or fair that takes place near you. At these events you'll find the widest array of different toys and trinkets... and because you're there in person you'll be able to evaluate the size and the quality of any item before you buy. Not many sex shops have a decent selection of BDSM toys, but if you're lucky enough to live close to one that does, this should be your first port of call.

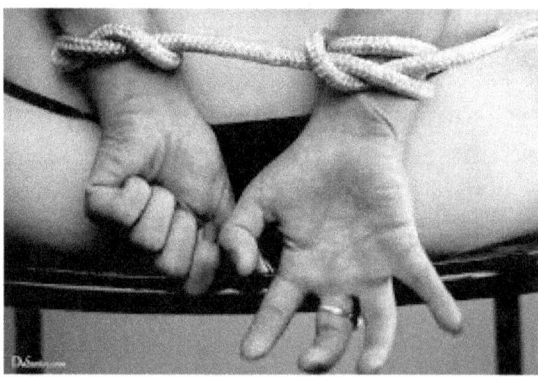

If you're not fortunate enough to live within practical distance of either an event or a regular sex shop, then you can still purchase toys online. It comes as a surprise to many that Amazon actually have a relatively wide range of toys on offer. Failing that Lovehoney and Uberkinky are both excellent and reliable suppliers... and they always use discreet and secure packaging as well. Read the online reviews of a given product before you buy, so that you know exactly what to expect when it arrives.

Try to purchase toys that are of good quality. Poor quality toys can be dangerous, and break easily. Breakages are not only frustrating and a waste of money, but they can also spoil an otherwise-excellent play session. High quality equipment might be slightly more expensive, but if you're buying an item that you plan to use frequently, the investment is certainly worthwhile.

Quite often, BDSM toys won't come with any kind of instruction manual. For this reason, take the opportunity when you purchase a new toy to find out from the seller what it's made from, and how you should take care of it. There may be certain cleaning products that you need to use or avoid, and – especially when it comes to insertables – it is often advisable to keep toys separate from one another. If stores together many soft or rubbery toys have tendency to melt and fuse; something that you'll certainly want to avoid.

While you may feel comfortable asking the seller how to clean and store your new acquisition, you might be rather less keen on asking them exactly how you're supposed to use it. Never fear, however – the internet is your friend. Whatever toy you've just acquired, there will be a guide (and probably a video) to its correct usage somewhere online. As before, by ensuring that you read up on things before you act, you will give yourself the gift of a much better play experience.

Bondage Tips

These next two sections are going to cover two of the most common activities that kinksters engage in: bondage and roleplay.

These by no means have to be your starting point when you feel ready to play, but they're good ways to shift away from vanilla sex and start exploring your fantasies... and it helps that you need very little equipment for either.

Bondage, for example, can be achieved with something as simple as a pillow case. Fold it into a narrow strip and then wrap it around your partner's wrists and you'll find that you're able to pin their hands down with ease. Scarves, a folded pillowcase, or even a cloth can serve as a rudimentary gag or blindfold, and if you invest in some rope the possibilities become almost endless.

One fantasy in particular that appeals to a great many people is to be able to tie their partner down spreadeagle on a bed.

This is something that can be difficult to achieve if you have anything other than a magnificent four-poster... but there is one very simple trick that will work on most beds. Simply take a length of rope, secure one end to one your partner's wrists and then run the rest of the rope all the way under the bed to the other side, where you can cinch their other wrist in place too. Do the same for their ankles, and your partner will be spread-eagled and unable to escape.

Do bear in mind, of course, that rope comes with its own set of dangers. Ensure that whenever you tie up your partner their bonds are not so tight as to cause pain or a loss of sensation. Have shears or a safety knife ready to cut them free if they get into difficulty. And if you're combining bondage with a gag or other impediment then make sure you've agreed a safe signal rather than a safe word with your partner, so that they can indicate if they need the scene to stop even if they are unable to speak. Safe signals can be as simple as a shake of the head, or as elaborate as giving your partner something to hold, and telling them to drop it if they need to stop.

If you want to learn about some of the more elaborate things that you can do with rope, then a simple online search for "**Shibari**" should send you in the right direction. This is the name given to the art of elaborate and aesthetically-pleasing bondage pioneered in Japan. It's immensely popular in the BDSM scene, and if you're lucky you might find that there are events local to you where you can learn and practice your skills with others.

Role Play

In a sense, all of BDSM is role play. One partner is playing the role of the dominant, while the other is playing the role of the submissive. There are, however, endless permutations of roleplay possible. Some of the more common ones you might already have thought of: a strict teacher and a naughty student, a doctor and their patient, a prisoner and their guard. A key element of good role play is that it allows the players to leave their normal identities behind. Quite often, by stepping out of their normal selves, they are able also to abandon some of their inhibitions, and give themselves over fully to the scene.

To help your first few role play sessions go smoothly, it's advisable to talk them over beforehand with your partner. Find a scenario that you both find appealing, and then discuss why you find it appealing. What exactly do you or your partner want from this scene? Which aspects of the scenario that you've picked do you both enjoy, and which aspects would you rather leave aside for now?

If you're a little self-conscious about giving yourself over to the role, then try adding in a few physical props. A costume, some bondage or a distinctive item can make all the difference. It also helps to begin the scene at a fairly low intensity – even jokingly at first... before pushing your way towards a more serious scene as you get used to your roles and the way you interact with one another.

Another trick for conquering self-consciousness is to write down your fantasy. Describe the situation you want to role play in words, and then give this written cheat sheet to your partner. They'll be able to read it, absorb it and understand your desires, and then step into the role that you've outlined.

If you're keen to try roleplay, but don't know where to start, try discussing the following scenarios with your partner to see what generates a spark:

- A doctor examining a patient... very closely indeed.

- A teacher disciplining a naughty student.

- A lone driver picking up a hitchhiker on the road.

- A secretary called into her boss's office for a private dressing down.

- A maid or manservant arriving to clean while the owner of the house sips a glass of wine.

Although these can sound cheesy at first, there should be something there to stimulate your imagination. And once you've started role-playing you'll find that it's addictive. There are few better ways to get your fantasies out of your head and into the real world than by sharing them with your partner in a role play session.

A Final Word…

That's as far as this guide goes, but this is only the beginning of your journey into kink. In the last few pages we've looked at how to play safely, how to improvise toys, how to start building your collection and how to enjoy both bondage and roleplay. You have inside your head now all the material you need to become a seasoned kinkster, with many years of happy play under your belt. Don't stop here. Head out and explore, and make sure you have fun while doing so. After all, at the end of the day, fun is what it's all about.